er own pace—in terms of
reading. Penguin Young
Readers recognizes this fact. As a result, each Penguin Young Readers
book is assigned a traditional easy-to-read level (1–4) as well as a
Guided Reading Level (A–P). Both of these systems will help you choose
the right book for your child. Please refer to the back of each book
for specific leveling information. Penguin Young Readers features
esteemed authors and illustrators, stories about favorite characters,
fascinating nonfiction, and more!

Giraffes

LEVEL 3

GUIDED READING LEVEL **K**

This book is perfect for a **Transitional Reader** who:
- can read multisyllable and compound words;
- can read words with prefixes and suffixes;
- is able to identify story elements (beginning, middle, end, plot, setting, characters, problem, solution); and
- can understand different points of view.

Here are some **activities** you can do during and after reading this book:
- Captions: Throughout the book, photos help show what's happening in the story. Go through the book and have the child pick five photos. Then have the child write a caption for each photo explaining what is happening. For instance, on page 16, the caption might be, "A giraffe eats acacia leaves."
- Research: The author writes that oxpeckers ride on giraffes and warn them about danger. Research oxpeckers. How do giraffes help them? What is this type of relationship called?

Remember, sharing the love of reading with a child is the best gift you can give!

—Bonnie Bader, EdM
  Penguin Young Readers program

*Penguin Young Readers are leveled by independent reviewers applying the standards developed by Irene Fountas and Gay Su Pinnell in *Matching Books to Readers: Using Leveled Books in Guided Reading*, Heinemann, 1999.

For Ailyn —JD

PENGUIN YOUNG READERS
An Imprint of Penguin Random House LLC

Photo credits: cover: © Thinkstock/Omelchenko; page 3: © Thinkstock/Omelchenko; page 4: (elephant) © Thinkstock/TobiasBischof, (lion) © Thinkstock/Eric Isselée, (zebra) © Thinkstock/prapassong; page 5: © Thinkstock/dmodlin01; pages 6–7: © Thinkstock/Bernhard Richter; page 8: © SuperStock/robertharding; page 9: (pattern) © Thinkstock/in_dies_magis, (vase) © SuperStock/Heritage; pages 10–11: © Thinkstock/CornelisNienaber_; pages 12–13: © Thinkstock/Anup Shah; pages 14–15: (pattern) © Thinkstock/in_dies_magis, (giraffe) © Thinkstock/Ilza; pages 16–17: © Thinkstock/BloomsCoffee; pages 18–19: © Thinkstock/anopdesignstock; page 20: © SuperStock/Biosphoto; page 21: © SuperStock/Roger de la Harpe; pages 22–23: (pattern) © Thinkstock/in_dies_magis, (giraffe) © Thinkstock/JHVEPhoto; pages 24–25: © Thinkstock/Johan_Kok; pages 26–27: © SuperStock/Thomas Dressler; page 28: © Thinkstock/JohnCarnemolla; pages 29, 34, 46: © Thinkstock/in_dies_magis; page 30–31: © 123RF Limited/Diana Amster; page 32: © Thinkstock/phatthanit_r; page 33: © Thinkstock/Valerii Kaliuzhnyi; page 35: © Thinkstock/Jameson Weston; pages 36–37: © Thinkstock/nup Shah; page 38: (top) © Thinkstock/sduben; (middle) © Thinkstock/Byrdyak; (bottom) © Thinkstock/mtcurado; page 39: © Thinkstock/Achim Prill; pages 40–41: © Thinkstock/Anup Shah; pages 42–43: © Thinkstock/Wassiliy; pages 44–45: © SuperStock/John Warburton Lee; page 47: © SuperStock/Marka; page 48: © Thinkstock/Fuse.

Text copyright © 2016 by Jennifer Arena. All rights reserved. Published by Penguin Young Readers, an imprint of Penguin Random House LLC, 345 Hudson Street, New York, New York 10014. Manufactured in China.

Library of Congress Cataloging-in-Publication Data is available.

ISBN 978-0-448-48969-8 (pbk)   10 9 8 7 6 5 4 3 2 1
ISBN 978-0-448-48970-4 (hc)   10 9 8 7 6 5 4 3 2 1

Giraffes

by Jennifer Dussling

Penguin Young Readers

An Imprint of Penguin Random House

Elephants. Lions. Zebras.

Africa has lots of cool animals.

And one of the coolest?

Giraffes.

Thousands of years ago, people painted giraffes on cave walls. Some people in Africa danced a giraffe dance to heal the sick.

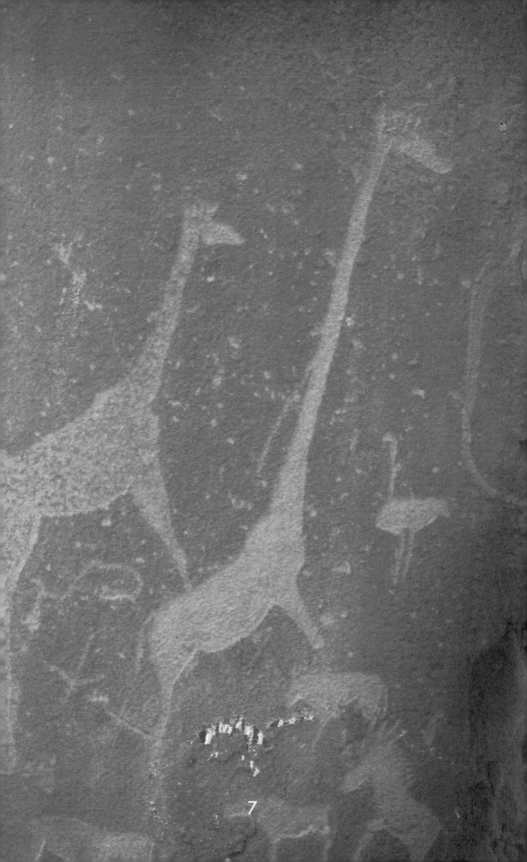

In Egypt, giraffes were kept as pets.
Romans thought giraffes were a mix
of two animals—a camel and
a leopard.

That's not true.

Back then, people didn't know much

about giraffes!

Today we know more.

But we still have a lot to learn.

Giraffes are the tallest animals
in the world.

Male giraffes can grow up to
19 feet tall.

Their necks are 7 feet long.

A neck like that must have
lots of bones, right?

No.

A giraffe has seven bones in its neck.

That's the same number of bones

you have in your neck.

But each giraffe neck bone is
about a foot long.

Long necks help giraffes reach food.

They eat leaves from acacia trees

(say: uh-KAY-sha).

The acacia trees are full of sharp

thorns.

A giraffe gets past the thorns with its

tongue.

A giraffe's tongue is 18 inches long.

It's also blue black!

A giraffe doesn't drink much.
Most of the water a giraffe needs
comes from acacia leaves.
That's good.
Bending down to drink is awkward
for a giraffe.
It can also be dangerous.

That's when lions attack!

What else do giraffes have
to worry about?
Hyenas, leopards, crocodiles.
These animals feed on giraffes.

Luckily, giraffes live in herds.
A herd usually has around
20 to 30 giraffes.
While some giraffes drink,
others keep watch.

Giraffes are good at keeping watch.

They have big eyes

with long eyelashes.

They have good eyesight

and good hearing.

They can spot danger from far away.

Oxpeckers keep watch, too.
The birds ride on a giraffe's
back or neck.

If one sees a threat, it makes a noise.
It's helpful when
the giraffe is napping.
Giraffes don't sleep much—
only 5 to 30 minutes a day!

Giraffes are gentle.

But they are not defenseless.

They run fast—up to 35 miles
per hour.

They have hard hooves.

A kick from an angry giraffe
can kill a lion!

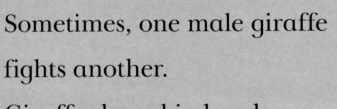

Sometimes, one male giraffe
fights another.
Giraffes have big heads
and heavy skulls.

Two males swing their heads
at each other.
They try to knock each other over.
This is called "necking."
They fight for the right to mate
with a female.

This female giraffe is about to give birth.

She leaves the herd to be alone.

She doesn't lie down.

She doesn't bend her legs.

Then—*thump!*

Her baby drops six feet to the ground.

What a rough way to start life!

Most baby animals are small.

Not this one!

A baby giraffe is as tall as

a full-grown man.

It weighs 150 pounds.

It has furry horns, too.

The horns are called ossicones

(say: oss-seh-kohns).

In an hour, the baby giraffe is on its feet.

For the first few weeks, the mother
and baby giraffe keep to themselves.
Then they join the herd.
The other giraffes greet them.
Giraffes are friendly.
They nuzzle.
They rub necks.
They watch out for one another.
When the mother giraffe needs
to find food, a giraffe "auntie"
helps out.
She watches the baby
until the mother comes back.

Look at the spots on a giraffe.

The spots are like fingerprints.
No two giraffes have
the same markings.
The pattern won't change for the
giraffe's whole life.

But different types of giraffes have different-looking spots.

 These spots look like a net.

These look like leaves.

 These have lots of bumps.

You can tell what kind of giraffe it is by its spots.

Why do giraffes have spots?

The pattern helps giraffes hide
in the wild.

They blend into sunlight and shade.

For a long time, people thought giraffes didn't make noises. But they do.
They snort.
They hiss.
Sometimes giraffes tilt their heads back.

Air rushes out of their throats.
The sounds are too low
for people to hear,
but machines can record them.
Maybe this is how giraffes "talk"
to one another!

Until 100 years ago, giraffes were
spread out in Africa.
But homes were built
where they lived.
Giraffes caught diseases
from farm animals.
Poachers trapped them.
Hunters killed them.

Many giraffes now live in national parks.

If you went to Kenya in Africa,
you could stay at Giraffe Manor.
Giraffe Manor is a hotel
on over 100 acres of land.

It's also home to a herd of giraffes.

The giraffes don't mind sharing
with guests.
They poke their heads
into the hotel's windows.
They watch people eat breakfast.
The giraffes are hoping for a treat!
Giraffe Manor is a safe place
for giraffes to live.
It's a great place to learn about
giraffes, too.

We still have a lot to learn
about giraffes.
They are tall.
They are quiet.
And they are really cool.